Student Guitar Etudes
Volume 1
by William Bay

WILLIAM
BAY MUSIC

Visit us on the Web at www.williambaymusic.com

Preface

The etudes in this book are melodic and guitaristic. I composed them in guitar friendly keys. They were written to be fun to play and also to provide short pieces ideal for recitals or concert preludes and encores. The pieces should be played with freedom and expression. I hope you enjoy playing these etudes. A special thanks to Ben Bolt for proof-reading my manuscript.

William Bay

Contents

Etude One/ E minor

William Bay

3

Etude Two/ C minor

William Bay

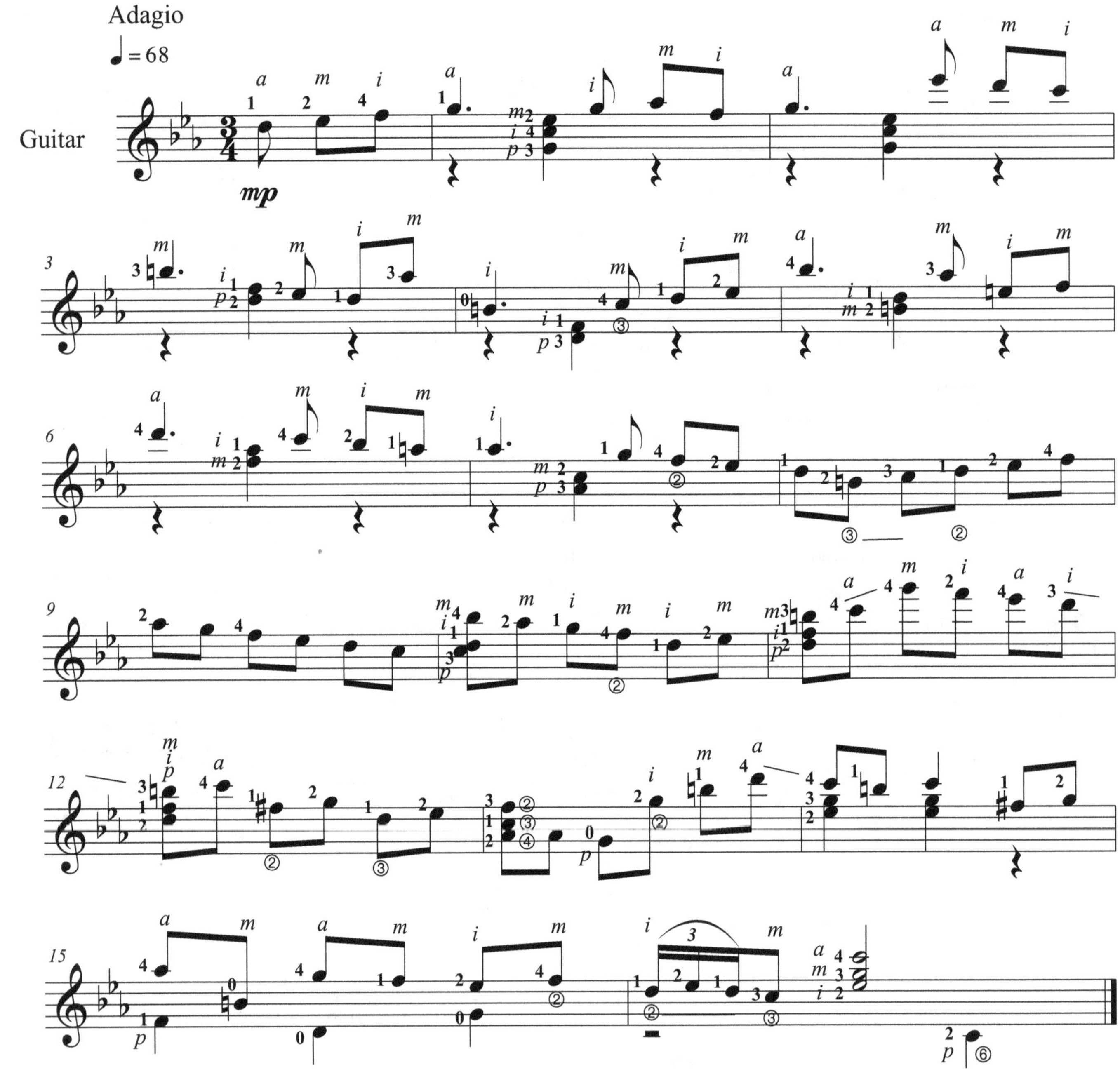

Etude Three/ E minor

Andante

William Bay

Guitar

5

Etude Four/ A Major

Allegro

♪=162

6

Etude Five/ E minor

William Bay

Moderato ♩ = 116

© 2012 by William Bay. All Rights Reserved. BMI.

7

Etude Six/ E minor

William Bay

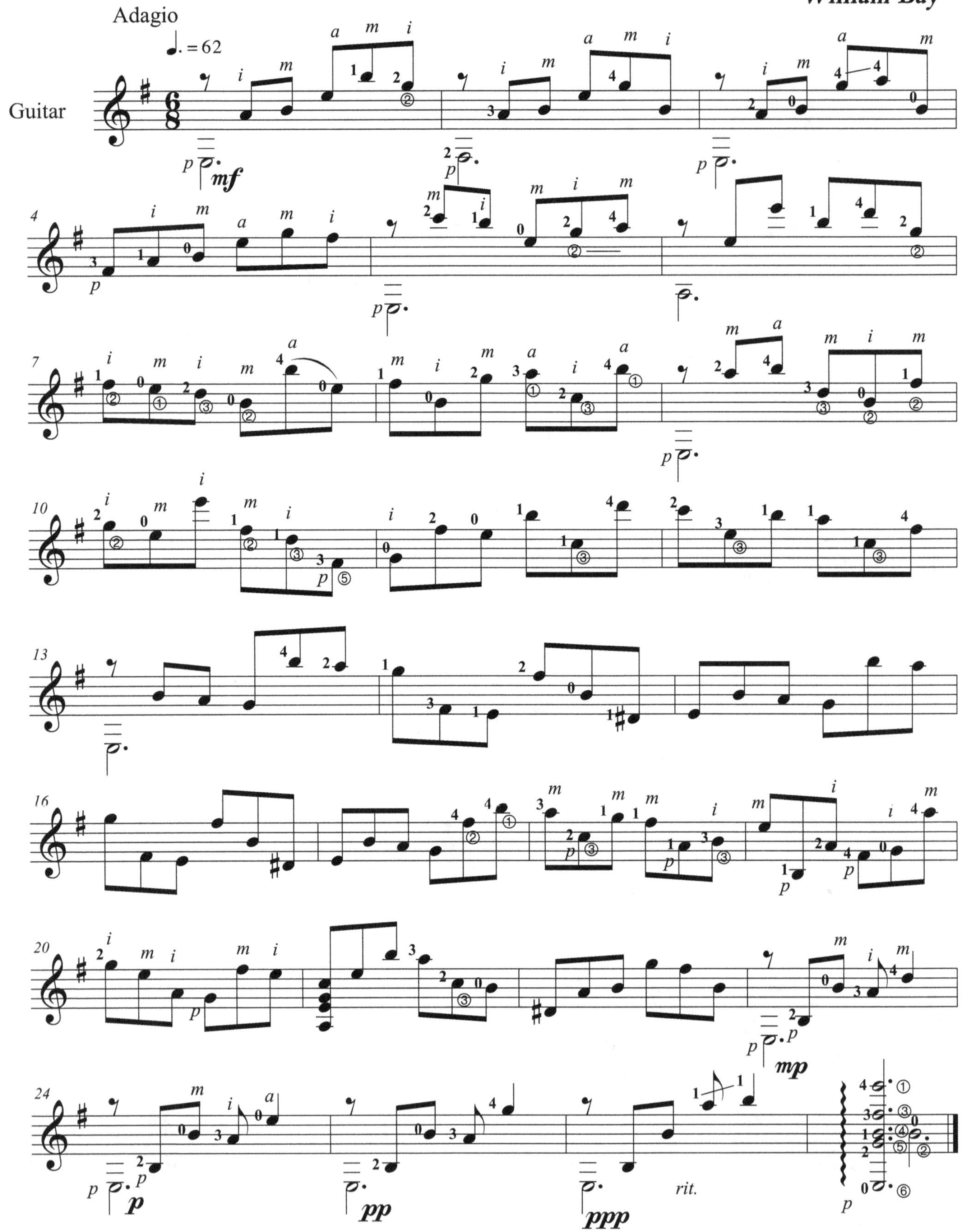

Etude Seven/ D Major

William Bay

Etude Eight/ A Major

William Bay

Moderato ♩ = 106

10

Etude Nine/ E minor

William Bay

Andante

♩ = 84

Guitar

Etude Ten/ D Major

William Bay

⑥ = D

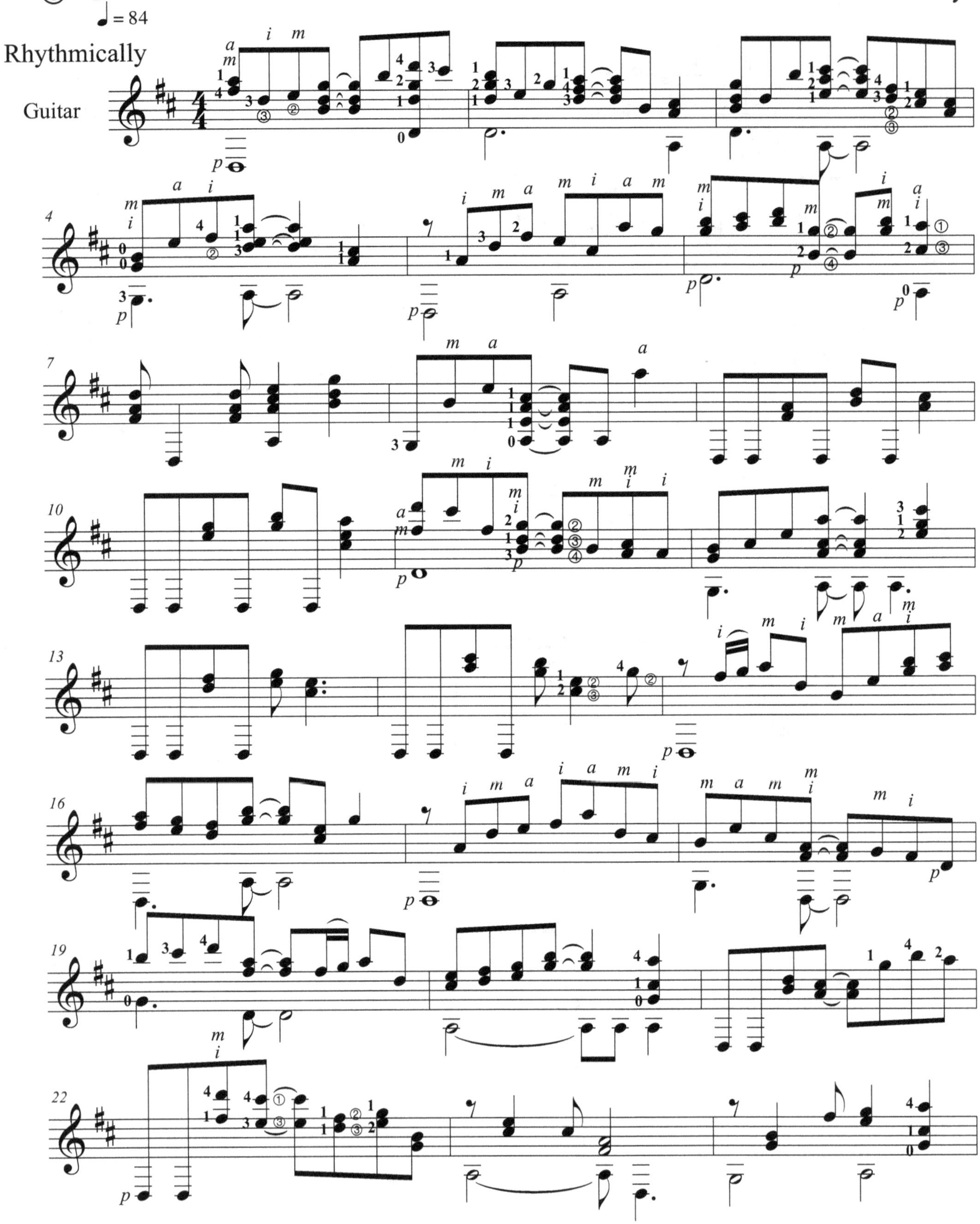
♩ = 84
Rhythmically
Guitar

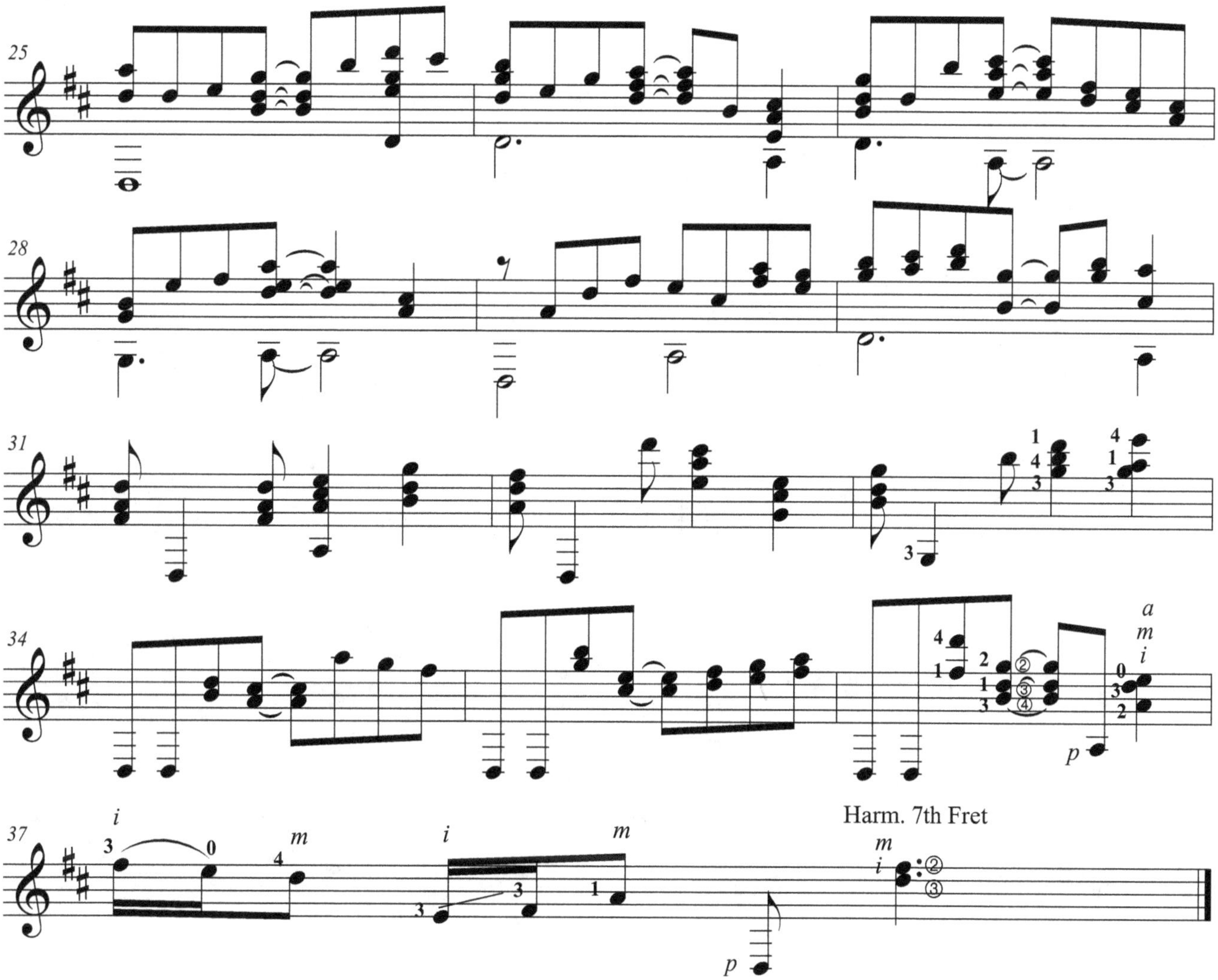
Harm. 7th Fret

Etude Eleven/ E Major

William Bay

Andante

♩ = 80

Guitar

Etude Twelve/ A Major

Andante

♩ = 84

William Bay

Etude Thirteen/ D minor

Dropped D Tuning

William Bay

⑥ = D

♩ = 80
Moderato

Guitar

16

Etude Fourteen/ E minor

Presto

William Bay

17

Etude Fifteen/ A Major

Moderato

♩ = 112

William Bay

18

Etude Sixteen/ C minor

Andante

♩ = 100

Etude Seventeen/ C Major

William Bay

Andante

♩ = 90

Guitar

21

Etude Eighteen/ D minor

William Bay

Dropped D Tuning

⑥ = D

Allegro ♪ = 158

Guitar

22

Etude Nineteen/ D minor

Dropped D Tuning
⑥ = D

Larghetto

William Bay

Etude Twenty/ E Major

William Bay

Adagio

24

www.ingramcontent.com/pod-product-compliance
Lightning Source LLC
Chambersburg PA
CBHW081453070426
42452CB00042B/2722